CHI

P9-CSE-976

Mid-Atlantic

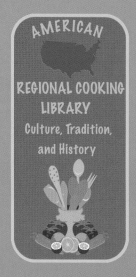

AMERICAN

REGIONAL COOKING
LIBRARY
Culture, Tradition,
and History

African American
American Indian
Amish and Mennonite
California
Hawaiian
Louisiana
Mexican American
Mid-Atlantic
Midwest
New England
Northwest
Southern
Southern Appalachia
Texas
Thanksgiving

Mid–Atlantic

Mason Crest Publishers
Philadelphia

Mason Crest Publishers Inc.
370 Reed Road
Broomall, Pennsylvania 19008
(866) MCP-BOOK (toll free)
www.masoncrest.com

First printing
1 2 3 4 5 6 7 8 9 10

ISBN 1-59084-618-4
ISBN 1-59084-609-5 (series)

Library of Congress Cataloging-in-Publication Data

Libal, Joyce.
  Mid-Atlantic cooking / compiled by Joyce Libal.
     p. cm. — (American regional cooking library)
  Includes index.
  ISBN 1-59084-618-4
  1. Cookery, American—Juvenile literature. 2. Cookery—Middle Atlantic States—Juvenile literature. I. Title. II. Series.
  TX715.L675 2005
  641.5974—dc22
                              2004010349
Compiled by Joyce Libal
Recipes by Patricia Therrien
Recipes tested and prepared by Bonni Phelps
Produced by Harding House Publishing Services, Inc., Vestal, New York.
Interior design by Dianne Hodack.
Cover design by Michelle Bouch.
Printed and bound in the Hashemite Kingdom of Jordan.

Contents

Introduction
by the Culinary Institute of America

Cooking is a dynamic profession, one that presents some of the greatest challenges and offers some of the greatest rewards. Since 1946, the Culinary Institute of America has provided aspiring and seasoned food service professionals with the knowledge and skills needed to become leaders and innovators in this industry.

Here at the CIA, we teach our students the fundamental culinary techniques they need to build a sound foundation for their food service careers. There is always another level of perfection for them to achieve and another skill to master. Our rigorous curriculum provides them with a springboard to continued growth and success.

Food is far more than simply sustenance or the source of energy to fuel you and your family through life's daily regimen. It conjures memories throughout life, summoning up the smell, taste, and flavor of simpler times. Cooking is more than an art and a science; it provides family history. Food prepared with care epitomizes the love, devotion, and culinary delights that you offer to your friends and family.

A cuisine provides a way to express and establish customs—the way a food should taste and the flavors and aromas associated with that food. Cuisines are more than just a collection of ingredients, cooking utensils, and dishes from a geographic location; they are elements that are critical to establishing a culinary identity.

When you can accurately read a recipe, you can trace a variety of influences by observing which ingredients are selected and also by noting the technique that is used. If you research the historical origins of a recipe, you may find ingredients that traveled from East to West or from the New World to the Old. Traditional methods of cooking a dish may have changed with the times or to meet special challenges.

The history of cooking illustrates the significance of innovation and the trading or sharing of ingredients and tools between societies. Although the various cooking vessels over the years have changed, the basic cooking methods have remained the same. Through adaptation, a recipe created years ago in a remote corner of the world could today be recognized by many throughout the globe.

When observing the customs of different societies, it becomes apparent that food brings people together. It is the common thread that we share and that we value. Regardless of the occasion, food is present to celebrate and to comfort. Through food we can experience other cultures and lands, learning the significance of particular ingredients and cooking techniques.

As you begin your journey through the culinary arts, keep in mind the power that food and cuisine holds. When passed from generation to generation, family heritage and traditions remain strong. Become familiar with the dishes your family has enjoyed through the years and play a role in keeping them alive. Don't be afraid to embellish recipes along the way – creativity is what cooking is all about.

Mid-Atlantic Culture, History, and Traditions

The Mid-Atlantic, a region that encompasses New Jersey, Pennsylvania, Delaware, Maryland, and Virginia, also surrounds the Chesapeake Bay, which was first explored by the Spanish in the middle of the sixteenth century. This area is an estuary, a place where the ocean's salt water meets fresh water, carried there by rivers. Approximately 150 rivers empty into the bay, but half the fresh water draining into the basin comes from the Susquehanna River. In the 1500s, the Spanish made a brief and unsuccessful attempt to establish a settlement on the York River, but American Indians were living on the bay long before the arrival of the Spanish. Indians called the Bay Chesepiooc, which means "Great Shellfish Bay."

Many tribes under the leadership of the Powhatan lived in the area between the Potomac River and what is now North Carolina. In addition to beans, squash, and corn (which were grown by many American Indian people), the Powhatans made use of the abundant oysters, crabs, and fish in the area.

In 1607, a group of English men arrived at the Chesapeake Bay, began exploring several tributaries, and established the Jamestown colony. The environment was harsh, and half of the original settlers were dead within the first year. In 1619, a Dutch ship carried the first African slaves to Virginia. Indentured servants had also been arriving to work for their freedom, but when the number of indentured servants decreased, people began purchasing slaves.

Mosquitoes thrived in the stale-water marshes surrounding Jamestown. By the end of the seventeenth century, the legislative assembly that had been established there decided to move to a more hospitable environment. Williamsburg (formerly called Middle Plantation) was the name given to the area where the state house was then established.

Two hundred immigrants arrived in 1633 and established the St. Mary's City settlement in the area now known as Maryland. American Indians, who called their town

Yowaccomoco, already inhabited that area, but they were bribed and coerced into abandoning their home. In both Virginia and Maryland, tobacco was the most important exported crop, and its production was a main reason for the use of slaves.

In the 1800s, coal was discovered in Pennsylvania, and a wave of immigrants from Germany, England, Wales, Ireland, and other European countries moved into the area. Many German immigrants settled in towns where they became shopkeepers and craftsmen, while immigrants from other countries often worked in the mining industry. Mining was a dangerous occupation, and child labor was common, with boys as young as nine spending long days in the dark caverns. Groups of families sometimes arrived and settled in an area together. Often they lived in housing owned by mine owners in small isolated communities called "patches." Women in these patches often worked together to care for children, bake bread, and tend gardens.

Like immigrants to other parts of North America, the immigrants to the Mid-Atlantic region brought their taste and knowledge of traditional foods with them. Today that heritage blends with the seafood culture of the Chesapeake Bay, as well the many fruits and vegetables grown locally. The result is the Mid-Atlantic cuisine this book explores.

Before you cook...

If you haven't done much cooking before, you may find recipe books a little confusing. Certain words and terms can seem unfamiliar. You may find the measurements difficult to understand. What appears to be an easy or familiar dish may contain ingredients you've never heard of before. You might not understand what utensil the recipe calls for you to use, or you might not be sure what the recipe is asking you to do.

Reading the pages in this section before you get started may help you understand the directions better so that your cooking goes more smoothly. You can also refer back to these pages whenever you run into questions.

Safety Tips

Cooking involves handling very hot and very sharp objects, so being careful is common sense. What's more, you want to be certain that anything you plan on putting in your mouth is safe to eat. If you follow these easy tips, you should find that cooking can be both fun and safe.

Before you cook...

- Always wash your hands before and after handling food. This is particularly important after you handle raw meats, poultry, and eggs, as bacteria called salmonella can live on these uncooked foods. You can't see or smell salmonella, but these germs can make you or anyone who swallows them very sick.
- Make a habit of using potholders or oven mitts whenever you handle pots and pans from the oven or microwave.
- Always set pots, pans, and knives with their handles away from counter edges. This way you won't risk catching your sleeves on them—and any younger children in the house won't be in danger of grabbing something hot or sharp.
- Don't leave perishable food sitting out of the refrigerator for more than an hour or two.
- Wash all raw fruits and vegetables to remove dirt and chemicals.
- Use a cutting board when chopping vegetables or fruit, and always cut away from yourself.
- Don't overheat grease or oil—but if grease or oil does catch fire, don't try to extinguish the flames with water. Instead, throw baking soda or salt on the fire to put it out. Turn all stove burners off.
- If you burn yourself, immediately put the burn under cold water, as this will prevent the burn from becoming more painful.
- Never put metal dishes or utensils in the microwave. Use only microwave-proof dishes.
- Wash cutting boards and knives thoroughly after cutting meat, fish or poultry — especially when raw and before using the same tools to prepare other foods such as vegetables and cheese. This will prevent the spread of bacteria such as salmonella.
- Keep your hands away from any moving parts of appliances, such as mixers.
- Unplug any appliance, such as a mixer, blender, or food processor before assembling for use or disassembling after use.

Metric Conversion Table

Most cooks in the United States use measuring containers based on an eight-ounce cup, a teaspoon, and a tablespoon. Meanwhile, cooks in Canada and Europe are more apt to use metric measurements. The recipes in this book use cups, teaspoons, and tablespoons—but you can convert these measurements to metric by using the table below.

Temperature
To convert Fahrenheit degrees to Celsius, subtract 32 and multiply by .56.

212ºF = 100ºC
(this is the boiling point of water)
250ºF = 110ºC
275ºF = 135ºC
300ºF = 150ºC
325ºF = 160ºC
350ºF = 180ºC
375ºF = 190ºC
400ºF = 200ºC

Liquid Measurements
1 teaspoon = 5 milliliters
1 tablespoon = 15 milliliters
1 fluid ounce = 30 milliliters
1 cup = 240 milliliters
1 pint = 480 milliliters
1 quart = 0.95 liters
1 gallon = 3.8 liters

Measurements of Mass or Weight
1 ounce = 28 grams
8 ounces = 227 grams
1 pound (16 ounces) = 0.45 kilograms
2.2 pounds = 1 kilogram

Measurements of Length
¼ inch = 0.6 centimeters
½ inch = 1.25 centimeters
1 inch = 2.5 centimeters

Pan Sizes

Baking pans are usually made in standard sizes. The pans used in the United States are roughly equivalent to the following metric pans:

9-inch cake pan = 23-centimeter pan
11x7-inch baking pan = 28x18-centimeter baking pan
13x9-inch baking pan = 32.5x23-centimeter baking pan
9x5-inch loaf pan = 23x13-centimeter loaf pan
2-quart casserole = 2-liter casserole

Useful Tools, Utensils, Dishes

barbecue skewers

basting brush

broiling pan

candy thermometer

flour sifter

food grater

hand juicer

slotted spoon

metal spatula

nut chopper

serrated knife

stock pot

wire whisk

Cooking Glossary

cream Mix an ingredient such as sugar or eggs into shortening until the mixture is light and fluffy.

cut Mix solid shortening or butter into flour, usually by using a pastry blender or two knives and making short, chopping strokes, until the mixture looks like small pellets.

dash Just a couple of drops or quick shakes.

deep fry To fry a food completely immersed in hot cooking oil or melted shortening so that all sides cook evenly and at the same time.

diced Cut into small cubes or pieces.

dredge To coat meat or seafood with flour or crumbs usually by dragging or tossing.

minced Cut into very small pieces.

sauté Fry in a skillet or wok over high heat while stirring.

shucked Sea food (such as oysters, clams, or mussels) with the shell removed.

simmer Gently boiling, so that the surface of the liquid just ripples.

steam To cook over just a small amount of boiling water.

whisk Stir briskly with a wire whisk.

Special Mid-Atlantic Flavors

bacon

Old Bay Seasoning

peanuts

white pepper

Mid-Atlantic Recipes

Bleenies

These potato pancakes are popular in the Mid–Atlantic States at church bazaars and block parties. "Bleenie lines" have been known to circle around the block.

Ingredients:

8 medium potatoes
1 medium onion
1 egg
4 tablespoons flour
salt and pepper
cooking oil

Directions:

Peel and grate the potatoes and onion. **Whisk** the egg, and stir in the vegetables, flour, and a *dash* of salt and pepper. Heat a little cooking oil in the skillet. Take a couple tablespoons of the potato mixture in your hands, flatten it, place it in the skillet, and fry until golden brown. Then flip it over, and fry the second side.

Tip:

Serve potato pancakes with jelly, applesauce, sour cream, maple syrup, or even a little vinegar.

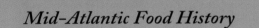

Mid-Atlantic Food History

Bleenies may take their name from Russian *blini*. These flour pancakes are so thin that you can almost see through them. Traditionally they were served with red caviar and a little butter, and they were loved by everyone from czars to peasants. Except in the fanciest restaurants, it is much less common in Russia to serve them with caviar now. Instead, they are paired with ground meat, cheese, fresh berries, or preserves.

Pancakes have an ancient origin, having been eaten in China as early as the fourth century B.C. People in India, England, Germany, Holland, Mexico, and many other countries have a history of eating pancakes. A Frenchman brought a recipe for *Crepes Suzette* to the United States in the 1930s. Toppings for these thin pancakes included butter, citrus juice, and sugar. This may be the recipe that led to the North American tradition of pouring maple syrup on pancakes.

Potato pancakes are part of many food cultures. For example, the Swiss eat a pancake made with shredded potatoes, the Norwegians call their potato pancakes lefsa, and Jewish latkes are traditionally served during Hanukkah and the Festival of Lights. Bleenies were probably brought to the Mid-Atlantic region by European immigrants.

German Potato Salad

This hot salad is popular in many areas that were originally settled by German immigrants.

Ingredients:

3 eggs
8 slices bacon
6 medium potatoes
1 large onion, chopped
3 tablespoons flour
½ cup cider vinegar
1 cup water
1 tablespoon sugar
½ teaspoon salt
½ teaspoon white pepper

Cooking utensils you'll need:
2 saucepans
skillet

Directions:

Place eggs and water in one saucepan, bring the water to a boil slowly, and boil 5 minutes. Drain, and cover with cold water. Peel the potatoes and boil them in the second saucepan until just tender. Drain, allow them to cool, and cut potatoes into ¼-inch-thick slices. Fry the bacon in the skillet until crisp. Remove the bacon, and place it on paper towels to drain off some of the fat. Discard all but 3 tablespoons of the bacon drippings. Cook the onion in the bacon drippings until tender. Add the flour, and cook, stirring constantly, until the flour begins to brown. Stir in the vinegar, water, sugar, salt, and pepper. Bring the mixture to a boil, and simmer until it begins to thicken. Meanwhile, peel and slice the hard boiled eggs. Place the potatoes and eggs in a serving bowl. Pour the hot dressing over all, stir, and serve.

Chesapeake Clam Chowder

Chowder is often served in East Coast restaurants and diners. This recipe comes from New Jersey, where there are so many diners that the state is sometimes referred to as the "diner capital of the world." You may already be aware of the two most well-known clam chowders—New England (white and creamy) and Manhattan (red because of its tomato base). With this recipe you get the best of both worlds— creamy chowder with diced tomatoes floating among the clams.

Ingredients:

3 or 4 medium potatoes
4 medium tomatoes
¼ pound bacon
2 medium onions, **diced**
24 chowder clams (reserve the liquid) (see "Tips")
1 teaspoon celery salt
½ teaspoon pepper
2 teaspoons Old Bay Seasoning
two 10½ ounce cans cream of asparagus soup
2 cups milk
1 pint light cream (half and half)

Cooking utensils you'll need:
measuring cups
measuring spoons
vegetable shredder
2 mixing bowls
sauce pan
serrated knife
stockpot

Directions:

Peel the potatoes, put them in the saucepan, cover them with water, boil until tender (about 20 minutes), and drain. When they're cool enough to handle, dice the potatoes, and set them aside. You need about 2½ cups for this recipe, but a little more or less won't hurt. Use the serrated knife to cut the tomatoes in half. Remove and discard the seeds, chop the tomatoes, and set them aside. Put the bacon in the stockpot, and cook until crisp. Remove the bacon, and place it on paper towels to drain off some of the fat. Add onion to the pot, and cook until tender and translucent. Stir in the clams with their juice, and heat. When they're hot, add the potatoes, celery salt, pepper, and Old Bay Seasoning. When all of that is hot, stir in the cream of asparagus soup, milk, and light cream. Bring the chowder to a gentle *simmer*, stirring occasionally to prevent it from burning. Add the tomatoes, continue simmering for 10 to 15 minutes, and serve hot.

Tips:

Steamed asparagus spears are a nice garnish for creamed soups and chowders.

To reduce the calories and saturated fat in creamed soups and chowders, replace some of the light cream or whole milk with fat free milk.

If you cannot find chowder clams in your grocery store, substitute 24 ounces of canned chopped clams.

Mid–Atlantic Food History

The first chowder recipe was published in 1751, but these creamy soups are much older than that. Undoubtedly, European immigrants already knew how to make chowders when they landed on North American shores. Indians living in coastal areas, however, probably made the first chowders on this continent.

Ingredients in chowders vary depending on the region of origin, but most recipes now include potatoes, onions, either bacon or salt pork, and some kind of fish or shellfish.

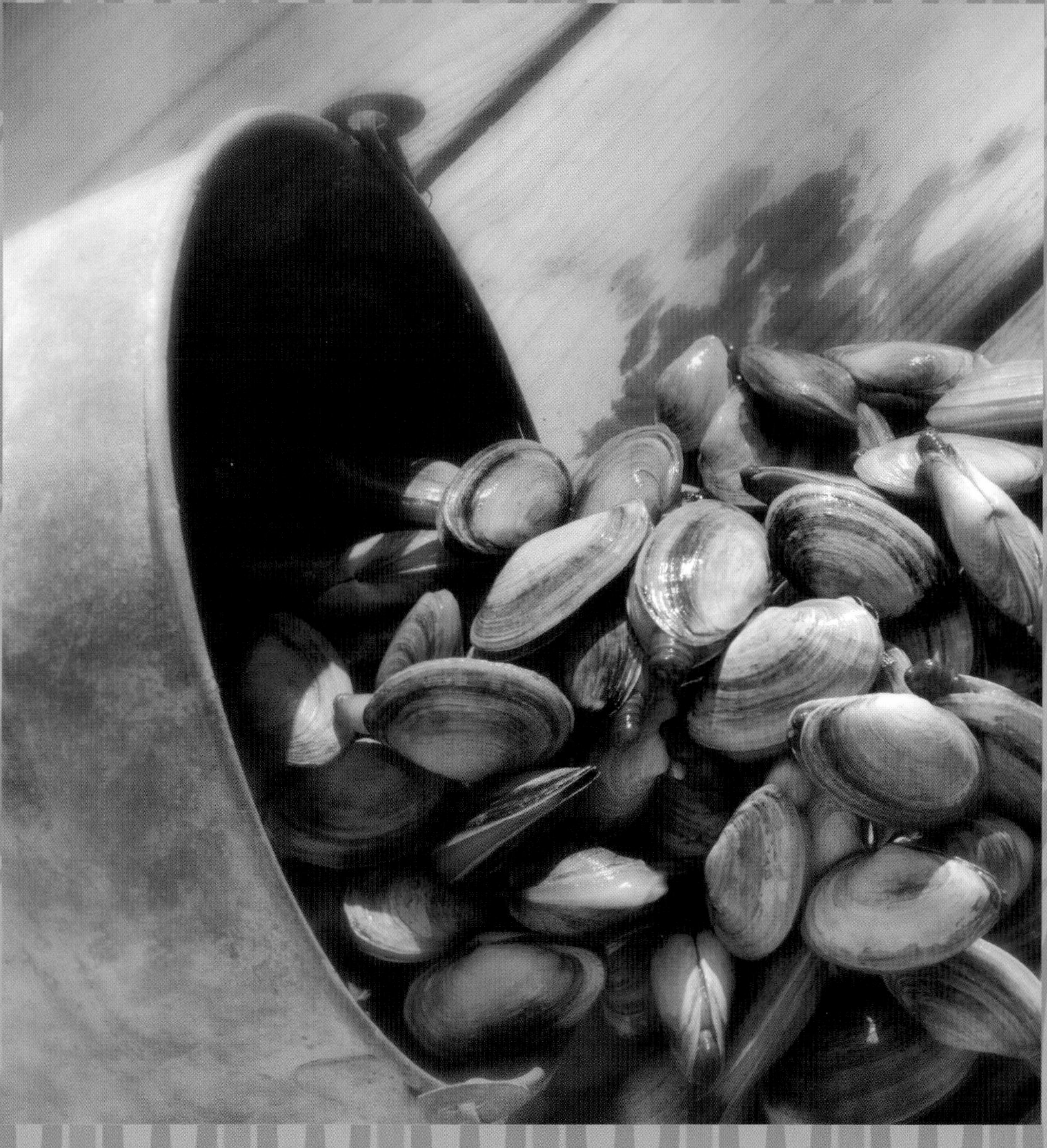

Cream of Crab Soup

Countless crab and oyster recipes are among the main contributions of Mid-Atlantic cuisine.

Ingredients:

4 tablespoons butter
1 teaspoon **minced** onion
1 teaspoon Old Bay Seasoning
1 tablespoon lemon juice
2 tablespoons flour
1 cup milk
1 cup light cream (half and half)
6 ounces crabmeat
fresh parsley

Cooking utensils you'll need:
measuring cups
measuring spoons
saucepan

Directions:

Melt the butter in the saucepan. Add the onion, and stir in the Old Bay Seasoning and lemon juice. Cook over medium heat until the onion is tender. Add the flour, and cook, stirring constantly, just until the flour begins to turn golden. Stir in the milk gradually. Stir in the light cream in the same manner. Add the crabmeat, and simmer for a couple of minutes to heat through and blend flavors. Garnish each serving with fresh parsley.

Tip:

Serve chowders and creamed soups with whole-wheat crackers or crusty breads and a vegetable or fruit salad.

Mid-Atlantic Food Culture

"Watermen" is a term exclusive to the Chesapeake Bay area and is used to describe people who make their living as fishermen. These people work long days using much the same equipment as their fathers and grandfathers. Though the meaning of the word changed, "watermen" is a term the immigrants to areas like Tangier Island in the Chesapeake carried with them from England. Other elements of speech have also changed little in the years since colonization in much of the Chesapeake Bay area. Watermen work year round beginning with fishing in the spring, crabbing in the summer, and harvesting oysters in autumn and winter. Clams and eels are also among the "catch" for many of these fishermen. African Americans also have a long history working as watermen.

Maryland Crab Cakes

Many people feel that Maryland blue crab is the best crab available.

Ingredients:

1 pound crabmeat
1 egg
¼ cup mayonnaise
1 teaspoon Old Bay Seasoning
2 teaspoons Worcestershire sauce
¼ teaspoon white pepper
1 teaspoon dry mustard
½ cup cracker or bread crumbs
cooking oil

Cooking utensils you'll need:
measuring cups
measuring spoons
mixing bowl
wire whisk
deep-sided pan for frying
candy thermometer
long-handled slotted spoon

Directions:

Whisk the egg with the mayonnaise, Worcestershire sauce, and seasonings. Remove any remaining cartilage from the crabmeat, and gently add it to the egg mixture. Stir in the cracker crumbs, and use your hands to make 6 crab patties. Put enough oil in the deep-sided pan to cover the crabcakes (see "Tips"), attach the thermometer to the pan, and bring the oil to 350° Fahrenheit. Use the slotted spoon to carefully place the crabcakes in the pan, and *deep fry* until they are golden brown (about 2 or 3 minutes).

Tips:

An alternative to deep frying for these crab cakes is to cook them in just 3 tablespoons of oil. When the first side is golden brown, flip the cakes over to cook the second side.

Serve crabcakes on a bed of mixed salad greens.

Crabcakes are delicious on their own, but you can also dress them with many different sauces, like mushroom cream sauce, roasted red pepper sauce, or even simple tartar sauce.

Mid-Atlantic Food Facts

Although the most successful area for harvesting blue crabs is the Chesapeake Bay, their range extends along the Atlantic coast from Nova Scotia to Argentina. Crabs grow larger by molting. This is accomplished by growing a soft new shell inside of the hard outer one. When the hard shell is first shed, the crustacean is known as a "soft shell crab." The entire body of crabs in this stage of development can be eaten and is highly prized as a delicacy. The shell immediately begins to harden, however, and within just 2 or 3 days, the animal is back to being a hard-shell crab. You can purchase soft shell crabs for cooking either live or frozen. Hard shell blue crabs are sold live, canned, or as pasteurized crabmeat. The males, called "jimmys," are often sold fresh, and #1 jimmys are the largest. Females, called "sooks," are usually steamed, and then the meat is removed for canning or pasteurization.

When purchasing crabmeat, notice the color and smell. It should look white or almost white and smell fresh (mildly like the "ocean"). If you are unable to purchase Blue crab, you can substitute other types of crabmeat (such as red crab or king crab) in recipes.

Aerial view of the Chesapeake Bay area.

Sweet Pennsylvania Pretzels

Some people think pretzels may have come over on the Mayflower! The first commercial pretzel bakery was opened in 1861 in Lititz, Pennsylvania. The Reading Pretzel Machinery Company located in Reading, Pennsylvania (which calls itself the Pretzel Capitol of the World), developed the automatic pretzel twisting machine in 1935. There are many recipes for various flavors of pretzel. Here's a sweet one for you to try.

Preheat oven to 450° Fahrenheit.

Ingredients:

baking soda (for exact amount, see "Directions")
1½ cups very warm water
1 package of active dry yeast
¼ cup brown sugar, firmly packed
4½ cups flour
salt

Cooking utensils you'll need:
measuring cups
measuring spoon
mixing bowl
large saucepan
cookie sheet
long-handled slotted spoon

Directions:

Grease the cookie sheet, and set it aside. Using a one-cup measure, fill the saucepan with water, keeping the water a couple inches below the top of the pan. Add 2 tablespoons of baking soda for every cup of water you used. Set the pan of water aside. Put the 1½ cups of very warm water in the mixing bowl. Pour the yeast over it, stir to dissolve, add the brown sugar and 1 cup of the flour, and stir again. Stir in between 3 and 3½ more cups of flour. Set the pretzel dough aside for 5 minutes, then divide it into a dozen pieces. Use your hands to roll each piece into a rope, then form the rope into the shape of a pretzel. Bring the water in the saucepan to a boil. One at a time, place each pretzel in the boiling water, remove it after just 10 seconds, and place it on the cookie sheet. Sprinkle the pretzels with the salt, and bake for about 8 minutes (until they're as brown as you like them).

Shrimp Kabobs

These delectable morsels make wonderful party food. Paired with a salad and crunchy bread, they can even be a main dish.

Ingredients:

1½ pound raw shrimp (fresh or frozen)
4 slices bacon
one 4-ounce can button mushrooms
1 large green or red sweet pepper
3 tablespoons melted butter or cooking oil

Directions:

Cook bacon in the skillet over low heat until soft. When cool enough to handle, cut into 1-inch lengths. If shrimp are frozen, thaw by running them under cold water. Peel shrimp, and remove the black "vein." Wash the pepper, cut it in half, remove and discard the seeds, and cut into 1-inch squares. Place a piece of bacon, a button mushroom, a pepper square, and a piece of shrimp on a skewer. Repeat until the space on the skewer has been utilized. Fill as many skewers as possible. Melt butter and brush on the kabobs. Broil about 3 inches from the heat source until vegetables and shrimp begin to brown. This will probably take only 5 minutes or less. Watch them closely because shrimp can burn quickly. Baste again, turn the kabobs over, and broil until the second side is cooked. Serve immediately.

Cooking utensils you'll need:
skillet
skewers
broiler-safe pan
basting brush

Barbecued Shrimp

Shrimp and bacon are a favorite combination. Here's another way to pair their flavors.

Preheat oven to 450° Fahrenheit.

Ingredients:

16 large raw shrimp (fresh or frozen)
8 slices bacon
barbecue seasoning
Old Bay Seasoning (optional)

Cooking utensils you'll need:
skillet (optional)
broiler pan with rack (see "Tip")
toothpicks

Directions:

If shrimp are frozen, thaw by running them under cold water. Peel the shrimp, and remove black "veins." If the shrimp are not large, cook bacon in the skillet until it softens. This is not necessary when using large shrimp. (The reason for doing this is so that the shrimp and bacon will be done at the same time when baking them in the oven.) Cut each slice of bacon in half. Wrap each piece of shrimp in a piece of bacon, and secure it with a toothpick. Place them on the rack above the broiler pan, sprinkle both sides with seasonings, set aside for 15 minutes to allow the flavors to blend, and then bake for 10 to 15 minutes.

Tip:

If you don't have a broiler pan with a rack, set a baking rack inside of another large pan such as a jelly roll pan.

Oysters en Brochette

Ingredients:

24 **shucked** oysters (about 2 pints)
1 large red or green sweet bell pepper
8 slices bacon
½ cup butter
1 tablespoon Worcestershire sauce
⅛ teaspoon liquid smoke
1 tablespoon lemon juice
½ teaspoon garlic powder
¼ teaspoon salt
dash cayenne pepper (optional)
¼ teaspoon pepper
16 medium mushrooms
16 cherry tomatoes
hot rice
fresh parsley

Cooking utensils you'll need:
measuring cups
measuring spoons
skillet
saucepan
skewers
broiler pan or other broiler-safe pan
basting brush

Directions:

Cook rice according to package directions. If you are using canned oysters, drain and reserve the liquid. Wash the sweet pepper, remove the stem, discard the seeds, cut into 1-inch squares, and set aside. Cook bacon in the skillet until soft. When cool enough to handle, cut each slice into 8 equal-size pieces. Melt the butter in the saucepan. Stir in the next 7 ingredients, add the reserved oyster liquid, and cook for 5 minutes. Remove from heat, cool slightly, and stir in oysters. Alternate vegetables, oysters, and bacon on skewers. Lay the skewers across the broiler pan, brush with the remaining butter mixture, broil 4 inches from heat source for 3 minutes. Turn the skewers, baste again with any remaining butter mixture, and broil for another 3 minutes. Remove broiled ingredients from skewers and serve over rice garnished with parsley.

Mid-Atlantic Food History

People have been enjoying oysters since ancient times. Both the Greeks and the Romans used this food, as did the Indians living on the coasts of North America. The Lenni Lenape Indians of the Delaware Bay area used it as a staple food. Oyster harvesting endured a dramatic increase after the arrival of European settlers. From the beginning, Americans had a voracious appetite for oysters. Although an average serving today is usually a half dozen, early settlers ate them by the gross. That's equal to 144 oysters! The average coastal colonial settler ate 10 bushels of oysters per year! The immigrants who lived further inland also liked oysters, and they were able to include them at some meals thanks to the arrival of the food first via stagecoach and later by rail. As early as 1812 in Delaware, and even 1719 in New Jersey, laws were passed attempting to regulate fishing. Bilvalve, New Jersey, became the center of the oyster industry, and by 1886 eighty train cars full of oysters were departing from the area daily.

When fishermen from different areas fish in the same waterways, conflicts can occur, especially if the target species becomes scarce. This is what happened in the 1800s when fishermen in Virginia and Maryland could not agree on a dividing line between their fishing territories in the Chesapeake Bay and Potomac River. The Maryland Oyster Navy was formed in 1868 to try to enforce a fair and peaceful coexistence on the water. This conflict lasted in some form for almost a hundred years. In 1962, laws were finally enacted to settle the dispute.

Mid–Atlantic Food Facts

Like much other naturally occurring seafood, oysters have been over-harvested off the coasts of North America. Today an effort is underway to restore their bounty. Luckily, we can still obtain this food, however, because it is commercially raised on "oyster farms." It may sound like a new idea, but people have been raising oysters for over 2,000 years. Today, the United States is one of the largest producers of oysters in the world.

It takes three years to raise an oyster to marketable size. Most of the oysters taken from the Chesapeake Bay are harvested using a tool called "hand tongs." This is a tedious and difficult job. It takes skill to hold and maneuver this heavy, scissors-like, instrument in deep water. Dredges, which are easier to operate and harvest more oysters at one time, are also used in some areas, but they cause damage to fragile oyster beds, so their use is restricted.

Oysters were first sold only in the shell. Live oysters were put in crates and floated down rivers. In the late 1920s, this method was banned because of concerns over polluted waterways, and suppliers began shucking oysters prior to shipment. A great many African Americans did this job in the Chesapeake Bay area. Many also worked on oyster boats.

Oysters in a Potato Crust

The crispy coating on these oysters adds a delectable crunch to each bite.

Ingredients:

1 egg
1 tablespoon water
½ cup flour
½ cup instant mashed potato flakes
4 tablespoons butter
6 large **shucked** oysters

Cooking utensils you'll need:
measuring cups
measuring spoons
small mixing bowl
2 plastic bags
wire whisk
skillet

Directions:

To shuck oysters, see "Tips." ***Whisk*** the egg with the water, and set it aside. Put the flour in one plastic bag and the potato flakes in another. Put the oysters in the bag with the flour, and shake to coat them well. Melt the butter in the skillet. Dip each floured oyster in the egg mixture, then ***dredge*** them in potato flakes. Cook them in the hot butter, browning them evenly on all sides. (This can take less than 1 minute.) Place cooked oysters on paper towels to drain off some of the butter. Remove from the paper towels, and serve.

Tips:

To shuck oysters, wash them first. Then put a heavy glove on the hand you'll use to hold the oyster. Use an oyster knife, screwdriver, or can opener in the other hand to open the oyster. Remove each oyster from its shell.

Wash the bottom half of the oyster shells well after shucking, and place each cooked oyster back on a washed shell to serve.

Hush Puppies

These deep-fried little bits of cornmeal batter are a traditional accompaniment to fish.

Ingredients:

1½ cups cornmeal
½ cup flour
1 teaspoon salt
½ teaspoon pepper
1½ teaspoons baking powder
¾ cup **minced** onion
2 eggs
3 tablespoons cooking oil
½ to ¾ cup milk
cooking oil for frying

Cooking utensils you'll need:
measuring cups
measuring spoons
flour sifter or wire-mesh strainer
2 mixing bowls
wire whisk
deep-sided pan for frying
candy thermometer
long-handled slotted spoon

Directions:

Pour oil into pan to about 3 inches deep, attach the thermometer, and heat the oil to 365°. While the oil is heating to the desired temperature, sift the cornmeal, flour, salt, pepper, and baking powder into one mixing bowl, and set aside. *Whisk* the eggs, 3 tablespoons oil, and ½ cup milk in the second bowl. Pour the egg mixture into the cornmeal mixture, and stir just until moistened. If necessary, add a little more milk, but only add enough to make a stiff dough. Stir the onion into the batter, and use your hands to form and squeeze the dough into little 3-inch-long cylinder shapes. Use the slotted spoon to carefully place them into the hot oil, and *deep fry* until golden brown (usually about 3 minutes), turning them as necessary to brown all sides. Fry the hush puppies in batches, and place them on paper towels to drain off some of the fat.

Tip:

If you are frying fish for dinner, you can fry the hush puppies in the same pan as the fish. Hush puppies are especially good with catfish.

Mid-Atlantic Food History

Several folktales explain the origin of hush puppies; most involve the desire of cooks to quiet barking dogs. According to one story, Southerners used these morsels to quiet their dogs when Union soldiers were nearby. Another story says it happened at a more congenial fish fry when many guests arrived with dogs. Cooks who desired to quiet the barking and howling animals, tossed a little of the fish batter into the hot grease and then threw the morsels to the dogs while admonishing them to, "Hush, puppies."

Shepherd's Pie

Leftovers are great when made into this favorite old-fashioned dish.

Preheat oven to 350° Fahrenheit.

Ingredients:

2 pounds lean ground beef
1 onion, chopped
leftover vegetables of your choice (see "Tips")
2 cups leftover mashed potatoes
leftover gravy or white sauce

Cooking utensils you'll need:
skillet
casserole dish

Directions:

Cook the ground beef and onion in the skillet until the meat is browned. Drain off and discard the excess fat. Stir any cooked vegetables that you like into the browned meat. (Carrots, peas, corn, and sweet peppers are all good choices.) Continue cooking until the vegetables are warm, and pour the mixture into the casserole dish. Spread the mashed potatoes on top, and bake for 30 minutes. Serve with leftover gravy or white sauce (see "Tips").

Tips:

If you don't have leftover vegetables, add frozen vegetables to the meat.

If you don't have leftover mashed potatoes, boil a couple of potatoes for 20 minutes, and then mash them with a little butter and milk. You could also use instant potatoes for this dish. You can vary the flavor of the potatoes by adding a little garlic powder or shredded cheese. This dish is pretty if the potatoes are placed around the edge of the casserole and the center is left open. Garnish the center with fresh parsley before serving.

You can use leftover cooked roast beef in place of the ground beef.

To make white sauce, melt 2 tablespoons of butter in a saucepan, and add 2 tablespoons of flour. Cook just until the flour begins to turn golden, and gradually stir in 1½ cups milk. Continue cooking until thickened, and add salt and pepper to taste.

Mid-Atlantic Food History

English settlers brought this recipe with them to the Mid-Atlantic region. In England, pies were usually meat-filled (rather than fruit-filled, as we are more accustomed to thinking of pies). Shepherd pies were originally made from lamb and vegetables, topped with potatoes, while cottage pies were made the same way, but with beef. Settlers in Maryland and other areas of the Mid-Atlantic region began to refer to any meat and vegetable dish topped with potatoes as "shepherd's pie."

Mid-Atlantic Food Facts

This particular type of smoked ham is famous for its unique flavor acquired through a number of different processes that begin with the hog's diet. Among other things, these animals eat peanuts, which may effect the taste of the final product. The first step in the actual processing of the ham involves "curing." During this stage all the lean surfaces of the meat are rubbed with a "cure mixture." Although salt can be used for this purpose, the preferred mixture also contains sugar and saltpeter. After the initial application, the meat is held at a constant 36° to 40° Fahrenheit temperature. Seven days later, the cure mixture is applied again. After curing, the ham is immersed in cold water for an hour, scrubbed, and allowed to dry. This increases the effectiveness of the "smoking" that will follow fourteen days of extended curing at a temperature of 50° to 60° Fahrenheit. When the smoking finally begins, a cool hardwood fire (less than 90° Fahrenheit) is used to create thick smoke. Hams are hung in this environment for one to three days, during which their color changes to a nut-like brown. The final "aging" process lasts between forty-five and 180 days. During this time the hams are kept at a temperature ranging between 75° and 95° Fahrenheit. Proper air circulation and humidity are very important during this stage to prevent the meat from drying out or becoming moldy.

Virginia Ham

Preheat oven to 375° Fahrenheit.

Ingredients:

11-pound smoked Virginia ham
2 tablespoons brown sugar, packed
1 teaspoon ground cloves
1 tablespoon bread crumbs
3 tablespoons dry cooking sherry

Cooking utensils you'll need:
stock pot
small mixing bowl
baking pan

Directions:

Scrub the ham to remove any coating of seasonings, put it in the stock pot, cover with water, and soak in the refrigerator for 24 hours, changing the water three or four times during that period. When you are ready to begin cooking the ham, put fresh water in the stockpot to cover the ham, bring the water to a boil, cover, reduce heat, and simmer for 20 to 25 minutes for each pound of meat. (For an 11-pound ham, for example, simmer for between 3 hours and 40 minutes and 4 hours and 40 minutes.) Then cool until the ham can be handled, and remove the skin and excess fat.

Put the brown sugar in the bowl, stir in the ground cloves and breadcrumbs. Put the ham into the roasting pan, and press the sugar mixture onto it. Bake uncovered for 15 minutes (until the sugar is melted). Drizzle the sherry over the ham, and return the ham to the oven until hot. (Begin checking the ham after 15 minutes.)

Tip:

If you are unable to get Virginia ham in your area, substitute another cured brand.

City "Chicken"

Preheat oven to 350° Fahrenheit.

Ingredients:

½ pound pork
½ pound veal
1 egg
bread crumbs (seasoned or unseasoned)
3 tablespoons cooking oil
1 cup milk

Cooking utensils you'll need:
measuring cup
2 small mixing bowls
bamboo or wooden skewers
wire whisk
skillet
baking pan
aluminum foil

Directions:

Wash the meat, pat it try with paper towels, and cut it into 1-inch cubes. Alternating the two types of meat, place them on skewers. Pour about 1 cup of breadcrumbs into one of the mixing bowls, and set it aside. *Whisk* the egg in the remaining bowl, and set aside. Put the oil in the skillet over medium heat. Dip the skewered meat into the egg, then *dredge* with breadcrumbs, place in the hot oil, and brown all sides. Remove browned skewered meat from the skillet, and place it in the baking pan. Pour the milk over the meat, cover tightly with aluminum foil, bake for 1 hour, and serve hot.

Mid-Atlantic Food History

This recipe takes its name from a situation that occurred during the Great Depression of the early twentieth century. Chicken is now abundant in the Mid-Atlantic States and elsewhere, but during the Depression it was an expensive food. Resourceful cooks substituted other meat for chicken in recipes. Placing pieces of pork or veal on a skewer gave people something to hold on to and made the meat seem more like a real chicken leg.

Barbecue

If you're not from one of the Mid-Atlantic States, you may know this simple but tasty recipe as "Sloppy Joe's."

Ingredients:

1 pound lean ground beef
1 medium onion, chopped
¾ cup ketchup
1½ tablespoon vinegar
1½ tablespoon brown sugar, packed
1½ teaspoon mustard
salt and pepper
hamburger buns

Cooking utensils you'll need:
measuring cup
measuring spoons
mixing bowl
skillet

Directions:

Place the ground beef and onion in the skillet over medium heat, and cook until the meat has browned. Meanwhile mix the ketchup, vinegar, brown sugar, and mustard together. Stir the mixture into the browned meat, *simmer* about 15 minutes stirring occasionally, add salt and pepper to taste, and serve on hamburger buns.

Tip:

For a change of pace, serve yourself "Barbecue" on a toasted hard roll. Melted cheese is a nutritious topper, and pickles add a nice contrasting crunch.

Mid-Atlantic Food History

The exact origin of this popular way of eating hamburger is a mystery. Many people think the burger originated in Iowa, while others claim its beginnings lie as far south as Havana, Cuba. What we do know for certain is that frugal cooks were adding home-grown vegetables and other flavorings to ground beef during the years of the Great Depression. Popular "fillers" for beef that could be produced at home included bread, onions, sweet bell peppers, tomato sauce and ketchup, eggs, and horseradish. Worcestershire sauce and mustard were also popular flavorings. Printed recipes for Sloppy Joe's date back to the mid-1930s.

Philly Cheese–Steak Sandwich

The fame of this sandwich extends way beyond its South Philadelphia origins. Now you can make your own version.

Ingredients:

1 pound sliced cooked roast beef (see "Tips")
1 tablespoon butter
1 large onion, sliced thin (Sweet Spanish is a good variety for this sandwich)
1 sweet green or red pepper, sliced thin
4 French or crusty Italian rolls
4 slices provolone cheese (Mozzarella, American cheese slices, or Cheez Whiz® are alternatives)

Directions:

Cut the roast beef into very thin slices, and set them aside. Melt the butter in the skillet, and cook the onion and green pepper slices over medium heat until tender (usually about 5 minutes). Use the serrated knife to cut the rolls open, but do not cut all the way through. Place the roast beef slices and onion/pepper mixture in the rolls. Top the vegetables with cheese, and place the open sandwiches in the broiler pan. Broil about 5 inches from the heat source until the cheese is melted, close the sandwiches, and serve.

Tips:

Many people eat this sandwich with ketchup or pizza sauce. Sautéed mushrooms are another tasty and nutritious addition.

If you're using Cheez Whiz, melt it in the microwave before adding it to the sandwiches.

You can begin with uncooked rib eye steak for this sandwich. Slice the raw meat into very thin slices. It may be easiest to do this if the meat is partially frozen while slicing. After removing the onions and peppers from the pan, add 3 tablespoons of cooking oil and sauté the meat slices until cooked through.

Mid-Atlantic Food History

The first Philadelphia Cheese Steak Sandwich was made by Pat Olivieri in the 1930s. Mr. Olivieri sold sandwiches and hot dogs in a section of South Philadelphia inhabited by Italian immigrants. His grandson still sells Philadelphia Cheese Steak Sandwiches in the same part of town, but now they are also widely available across the city.

Many people think it is impossible to duplicate the exact taste and texture of the sandwich beyond the borders of Philadelphia because of the particular type of long, thin Italian roll available there. Also key is the incredible thinness of the beef slices, usually only one-sixteenth of an inch. Cheez Whiz has become the "cheese of choice" for this sandwich among Philadelphia residents. It is so popular that it has acquired the nickname "Whiz."

Brunswick Stew—Virginia Style

Although this recipe calls for chicken and ham, during colonial times, Brunswick Stew was made with wild game, such as squirrel. Some Virginians still include rabbit in the recipe.

Ingredients:

1 pound chicken parts
½ pound lean ham
1 large onion, diced
12 cups water
1½ pound tomatoes, diced
2 cups lima beans
4 large potatoes, diced
2 ears of corn (see "Tips")
1 tablespoon salt
¼ teaspoon pepper
1 small red chili pepper (washed but not cut)
2½ tablespoons butter

Cooking utensils you'll need:
measuring cups
measuring spoons
stockpot

Directions:

Wash the meat, and pat it dry with paper towels. Cut the ham into small pieces. Place the meat, onion, and water in the stockpot, bring to a boil, cover, reduce heat, and *simmer* 2 hours. Put everything else, except the butter, into the pot, and continue simmering, covered, for another hour. Stir often while cooking to prevent ingredients from sticking to the bottom of the pot. Stir in the butter just before serving.

Tips:

To cut corn off the cob, hold it upright and steady with the stem side down. With a sharp knife in your other hand, slice downward, cutting off a few rows of corn kernels. Then go back and gently scrape that area of the cob to get more of the corn juice. Some people like to place the cob in the center tube of an angel-food cake pan so the cut kernels fall into the pan. You still need to hold the cob steady as you cut when using this method.

If fresh corn is not available, use canned or frozen whole-kernel corn.

Handle fresh hot peppers carefully. Do not put your hands near your eyes when working with any food, but be especially careful when working with hot peppers. Always wash your hands with soap and water after handling these vegetables.

Mid-Atlantic Food History

The European origin of this famous stew may be in Braunsweig, Germany. King George II of England granted land in colonial America to immigrants from Braunsweig. When the colonists arrived in their new homes, they brought their food traditions with them. Three areas called "Brunswick," which is the English version of Braunsweig, now claim to have developed this famous stew (Brunswick, North Carolina, Brunswick, Georgia, and Brunswick County, Virginia). In Virginia, they say the stew was first made by a cook named Jimmy Matthews, who worked for Dr. Creed Haskins, a member of the Virginia House of Delegates. Mr. Matthews first made the stew between 1828 and 1830, using squirrel, bread, and onions. Several people ate the stew, and it became popularly knows as Brunswick Stew. Of course, American Indians were already eating similar stews long before 1828.

There are many versions of this stew. Some call for traditional Southern ingredients like shoe peg corn, fatback, and butter beans. Virginia Brunswick Stew is very different from Georgia Brunswick Stew, but both are thick and savory one-pot meals.

Bethlehem Cookies

Preheat oven to 350° Fahrenheit.

Ingredients:

7 cups four
2 teaspoons baking soda
2 cups shortening (Traditionally, these cookies are
made with lard.)
6 eggs
1 pint sour cream
1 box confectioners' sugar (powdered sugar)
ground nuts (poppy seed is another option)

Cooking utensils you'll need:
food processor or nut grinder
measuring cups
measuring spoon
2 large mixing bowls
2 small bowls
rolling pin
wooden cutting board (optional)
cookie sheet
plastic wrap

Directions:

Mix the flour and baking soda together in one mixing bowl, and set it aside. Put the shortening in the second mixing bowl, and set it aside. Using the two small bowls, separate the egg whites from the yolks. Use the whites for another purpose. *Cream* the egg yolks into the shortening. Stir in the sour cream. Add the flour mixture and stir well. Cover the bowl with plastic wrap and refrigerate for 2 hours. Preheat oven to 350° Fahrenheit. Spread some confectioners' sugar on a wooden cutting board or other flat surface and on the rolling pin. Sprinkle ground nuts or poppy seed onto the sugar. Using about 2 cups of the dough at a time, roll the dough about ⅛- to ¼-inch thick. Cut round cookies using a glass, being sure to dip the rim into confectioners' sugar between each cookie to prevent the cookies from sticking to it. Pick each cookie up with a metal spatula dipped in confectioners' sugar, and turn the cookie over so that the nuts or poppy seeds are on top as you place it on the cookie sheet. Bake for 10-15 minutes (until the tops of the cookies begin to turn golden brown).

Delaware's Cream Cheese & Pineapple Pie

Preheat oven to 400° Fahrenheit.

Ingredients:

⅓ cup and ½ cup sugar
1 tablespoon cornstarch
8 ounces crushed pineapple with juice
one 8-ounce package cream cheese
½ teaspoon salt
2 eggs
½ cup milk
½ teaspoon vanilla
1 unbaked pie shell (see "Tips")
¼ cup chopped pecans

Cooking utensils you'll need:
measuring cups
measuring spoons
saucepan
mixing bowl
electric mixer (optional)
nut chopper or knife to cut the nuts
pie pan

Directions:

Put the cream cheese in the mixing bowl, and set it aside to soften. Combine ⅓ cup sugar and the cornstarch in the saucepan. Stir in the pineapple and juice. Place over medium heat. Cook and stir until thickened, and set the mixture aside to cool. Using the electric mixer, beat one egg into the cheese. Repeat with the second egg. Beat in the remaining ½ cup sugar, salt, and vanilla. Gradually beat in milk. Pour the cooled pineapple mixture into the unbaked pie shell. Gently spread the cream cheese mixture on top, sprinkle with the chopped nuts, and bake for 50 minutes (until cream cheese mixture is set and beginning to turn golden). Serve the pie cooled, and refrigerate any leftovers.

Tips:

You could also make this pie with other canned fruit such as the sweet peaches grown in Virginia's Shenandoah Valley. Simply cut the fruit into small pieces before proceeding with the recipe.

If you want to try making your own piecrust, mix ¾ cup flour with ¼ teaspoon salt. Cut in 2 tablespoons shortening. When the mixture looks like meal, cut in another 2 tablespoons shortening. Cut in 1½ tablespoons cold water. Gather the dough into a ball. Sprinkle flour on a flat surface such as a wooden cutting board and on a rolling pin. Place the dough on the flat surface and pat it a little to begin flattening it out. Lift it up and put a little flour under it. Begin rolling from the center outward and in all directions. Add more flour to the rolling pin as necessary. Lift up the edges of the dough and add more flour if necessary. When the dough is the size needed for the pie plate, fold it in half. Place the pie plate next to the dough, slide the dough into it, and open the folded dough up. Gently pat the dough into the pie plate, crimp the edges of the dough, and trim off any excess with a butter knife.

Virginia Peanut Brittle

What makes peanut brittle "Virginia" Peanut Brittle? Virginia peanuts of course! Virginia Peanuts are one of four varieties grown in the United States.

Ingredients:

2 cups sugar
1 cup light corn syrup
1 cup water
2 cups unroasted, unsalted peanuts
¼ teaspoon salt
1 teaspoon butter or margarine
¼ teaspoon baking soda

Cooking utensils you'll need:
measuring cups
measuring spoons
12-inch deep-sided skillet
or other deep-sided pan
candy thermometer
2 jelly roll pans
metal spatula
butter knife

Directions:

Butter the bottom and sides of the jelly roll pans, and set them aside. Break up the peanuts so that they are not stuck together in pairs. Put the sugar into the skillet, and stir in the corn syrup and water. Look at the candy thermometer before attaching it to the pan. Notice where the soft ball and hard crack lines are located. Attach candy thermometer to pan, and cook over medium heat, stirring until the sugar is completely dissolved. Continue cooking until the mixture reaches 236° Fahrenheit (that is just under the soft ball stage of 240° Fahrenheit). Immediately stir in the peanuts and salt without removing the mixture from the heat. Continue cooking until the mixture reaches between 290° and 300° Fahrenheit (that is beyond the soft crack stage of 303°

Fahrenheit). Immediately stir in the butter and baking soda. (Do not be surprised when the mixture foams.) Immediately pour the candy into the buttered pans. Use a buttered metal spatula to loosen the peanut brittle along the edges and bottom of the pan. As the candy begins to firm up and is cool enough to handle, dump it out of the pans, and pull it with your hands to make the center thinner. Allow the candy to cool completely, and use the handle of the butter knife to break it into pieces.

Mid–Atlantic Food History

There are approximately 3,000 peanut farms in Virginia today—but where did peanuts first come from? They probably originated more than 3,500 years ago in Peru or Brazil. Ancient graves of the Moche and Inca people have been found that contain string bags and jars filled with peanuts. By 3,000 years ago, some of the people living in South America were already making peanuts into a kind of paste, and cocoa beans were sometimes added to the mixture. Peanut butter and chocolate were popular even then! Peanuts had already spread to Mexico by the time the Spanish arrived in the New World. Portuguese and Spanish explorers carried peanuts to Spain, Portugal, Asia, and Africa. In the Congo, peanuts were called nguba, and this is probably the origin of the word "goober," one of the terms that was later used for peanuts in North America. Peanuts were used as food aboard the slave ships that brought Africans to America. Once in America, Africans planted peanuts in many places in the South, but they were not eaten often by Anglo-Americans until the outbreak of the Civil War. Union and Confederate soldiers used them for food and sometimes ground them for use as a substitute for coffee. The popularity of peanuts began to rise after the Civil War, and in 1870, P.T Barnum's Circus began selling roasted peanuts. Virginia produced its first commercial crop of peanuts in the 1840s.

Further Reading

Cook, Anne Quinn. *Seasons of Pennsylvania: A Cookbook*. State College, Penn.: Pennsylvania State University Press, 2002.

Davis, William C. *Civil War Cookbook: A Unique Collection of Traditional Recipes and Anecdotes from the Civil War Period*. Philadelphia, Penn.: Courage Books, 2003.

Fullinwider, Rowena J., James A. Crutchfield and Winette Sparkman Jeffery. *Celebrate Virginia Cookbook: The Hospitality, History, and Heritage of Virginia*. Nashville, Tenn.: Cool Springs Press, 2002.

Hayes, Joanne Lamb. *Grandma's Wartime Kitchen: World War II and the Way We Cooked*. New York: St. Martin's Press, 2000.

McKee, Gwen and Barbara Moseley., eds., *Best of the Best from the Mid-Atlantic Cookbook: Selected Recipes from the Favorite Cookbooks of Maryland, Delaware, New Jersey and Washington, D.C.* Brandon, Mo.: Quail Ridge Press, 2001.

Otterbourg, Robert K. *Careers in the Food Services Industry (Success Without College)*. Hauppauge, New York: Barrons Educational Series, 1999.

Wood, Rebecca. *The New Whole Foods Encyclopedia: A Comprehensive Resource for Healthy Eating*. New York: Penguin Group, 1999.

For More Information

Chesapeake Bay History
www.mariner.org/baylink

Food History
www.kitchenproject.com

History of Immigrants to the Coal Region
www.amphilsoc.org/library/exhibits/wallace/immigrants.htm

Kitchen Safety
www.premiersystems.com/recipes/kitchen-safety/cooking-safety.html

State History
www.theus50.com

Publisher's note:
The Web sites listed on this page were active at the time of publication. The publisher is not responsible for Web sites that have changed their addresses or discontinued operation since the date of publication. The publisher will review and update the Web sites upon each reprint.

Index

Author:
In addition to writing, Joyce Libal has worked as an editor for a half dozen magazines, including a brief stint as recipe editor at *Vegetarian Gourmet*. Most of her experience as a cook, however, has been gained as the mother of three children and occasional surrogate mother to several children from different countries and cultures. She is an avid gardener and especially enjoys cooking with fresh herbs and vegetables and with the abundant fresh fruit that her husband grows in the family orchard.

Recipe Tester / Food Preparer:
Bonni Phelps owns How Sweet It Is Café in Vestal, New York. Her love of cooking and feeding large crowds comes from her grandmothers on both sides whom also took great pleasure in large family gatherings.

Consultant:
The Culinary Institute of America is considered the world's premier culinary college. It is a private, not-for-profit learning institution, dedicated to providing the world's best culinary education. Its campuses in New York and California provide learning environments that focus on excellence, leadership, professionalism, ethics, and respect for diversity. The institute embodies a passion for food with first-class cooking expertise.

Recipe Contributor:
Patricia Therrien has worked for several years with Harding House Publishing Service as a researcher and recipe consultant—but she has been experimenting with food and recipes for the past thirty years. Her expertise has enriched the lives of friends and family. Patty lives in western New York State with her family and numerous animals, including several horses, cats, and dogs.

Picture Credits

Corel pp. 9, 51, 68, 69

Photos.com cover, pp. 12, 15, 16, 18, 21, 22, 38, 39, 45, 52, 56, 72

PhotoDisc cover, pp. 19, 20, 46, 49, 59, 69

BrandX pp. 30, 42, 55

Corbis pp. 50, 68

Benjamin Stewart pp. 10, 23, 24, 27, 33, 37, 41, 60, 63, 64, 69

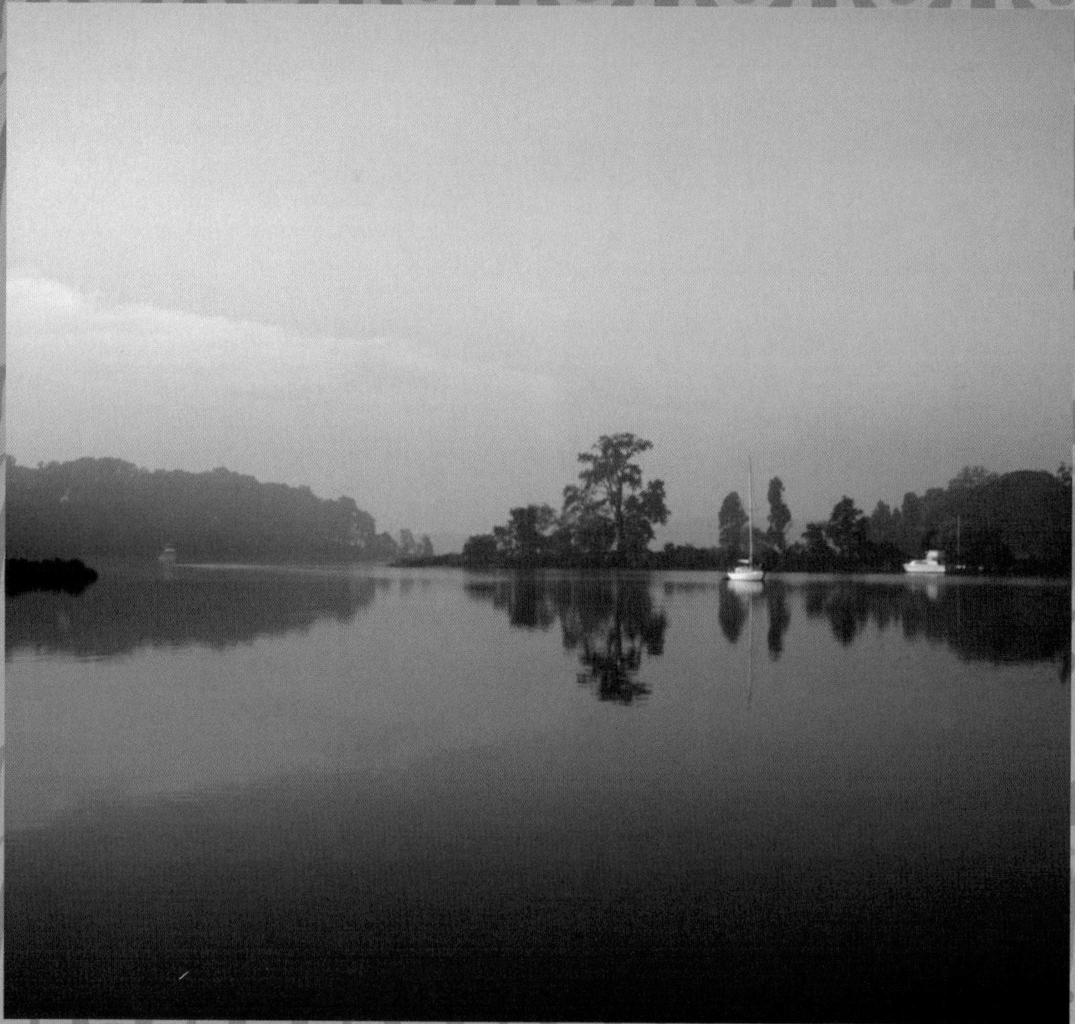